Just a kid, a canvas, and a dream

WRITTEN AND ILLUSTRATED BY JORDAN ARNELL EVANS

Author Jordan Arnell Evans c
2023 Art Jordan
All Reserved Rights
www.artjordan.net Follow
@artjordan_
Eztaughtme LLC

"Hi, I'm Hoggie!"

This story is about a kid named Hoggie. The name Hoggie comes from the nickname of the author Jordan Arnell, which was given to him by his family members as a kid. Hoggie is a kid artist discovering his talents and finding ways to use them in the real world. Hoggie meets a special friend who helps mentor him to become one of the best kid artists in the world. During this journey, he learns life lessons and what it takes to be a great artist. The mission may seem challenging, but knowing Hoggie, he will come out on top.

04-28-2024

I dedicate this book to my family, friends, my community and to those who have supported me without even meeting me. This one is for you!

Love,
Hoggie

One hot summer day, Hoggie left an art store with his mother. On the way out, they passed an art stand filled with supplies like pencils, paper, canvases, and paint. "Mom, can I have one of those canvases?" he asked. "No, not today, Hoggie. We will get one later," she said.

Hoggies mom then asked, "Hoggie, did you know that if you save all your money, you can buy all that on your own? You create the art, then resell it?" Hoggie thought about this for a minute, then said, "Mom, can I get it now? It will be worth it, I promise." Hoggie's Mom giggled and said, "I will get the canvas, but you must get the art supplies."

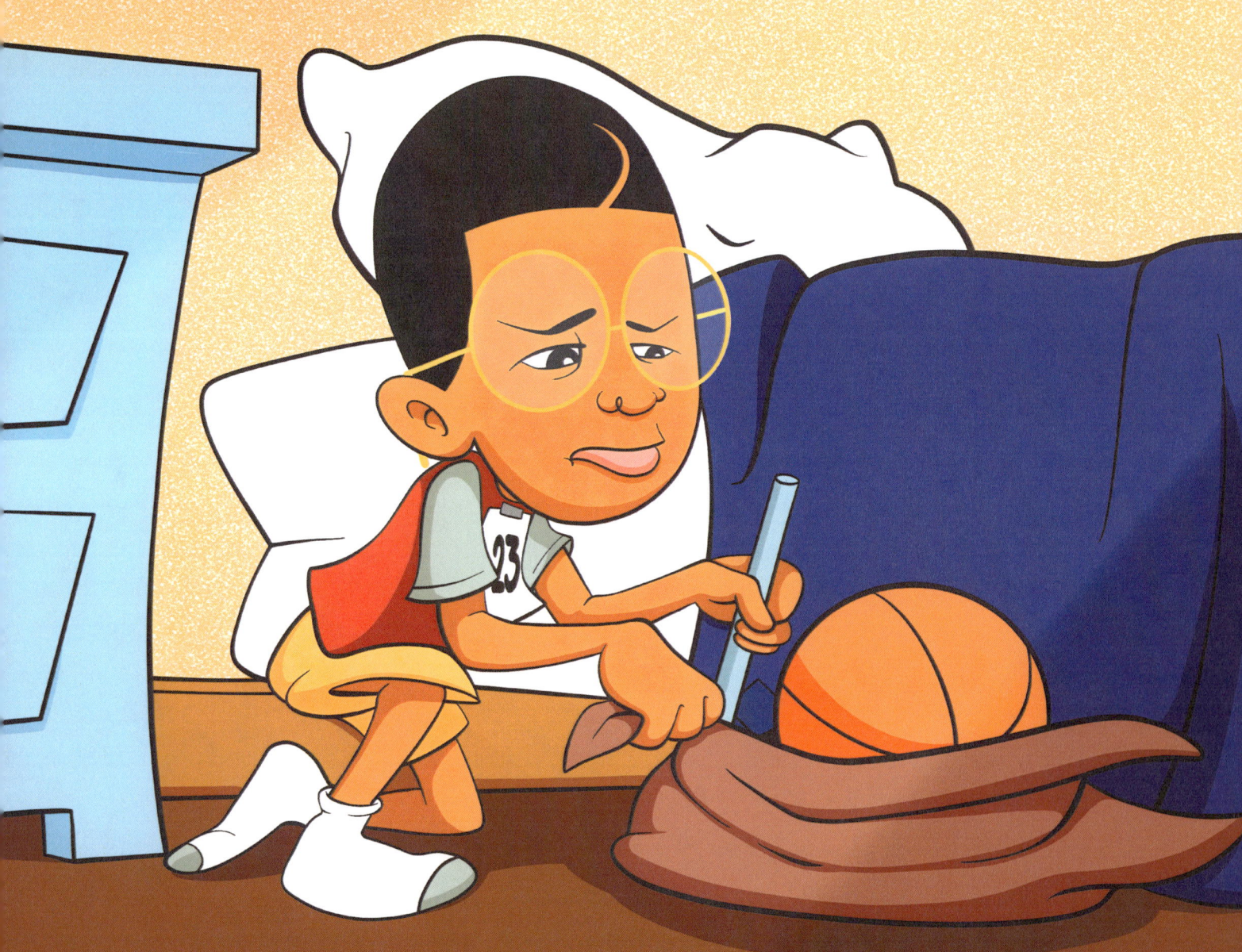

"Down here," said the voice. Hoggie began to move things around until he saw the canvas his Mom had just bought. The canvas began to speak again.

"Well," Hoggie explained, "My parents said I have to save my own money to buy my art supplies. I want to prove to them that I can, and can become the greatest artist in the world. The problem is, I don't know anything about getting money to buy my art supplies." Canvy smiled and said to Hoggie, "Don't worry, I know everything about investing! I'll be your mentor." "What's a mentor?" Hoggie asked.

"Sure!" Canvy said. Canvy asked Hoggie, "What type of artist do you want to be and why do you want to become an artist." Hoggie said, "I want to sell my artwork and I want to sell them on clothes too. I also want to become the most known artist in the world!" Canvy smiled and explained that this was not a good enough reason to be an artist. Hoggie thought some more, then said, "Well, I also want to make lots of money, be a leader in my community, and help other artists." "Now those are great reasons to become an artist!" Canvy said.

Canvy told Hoggie that the first thing he would need was a plan. "What's a plan?" Hoggie asked. Canvy explained. "It's a map that explains what you will sell and how much money you plan on making from the art. Canvy gave Hoggie a sheet of paper. "You can write down your plan and ideas on this sheet of paper." Canvy said. Hoggie wrote it down and showed it to Canvy. "Goooood," said Canvy. "Now let's see how much money it will take to buy these supplies.

So, Hoggie and Canvy got to work. After looking up prices for everything, Canvy said, "It looks like you will need $5000 to start which includes $1500 for the IPad, $1000 for canvases, $350 for the IPad case, $500 for paint, $100 for an apple pencil, $200 for t-shirts, and the rest we will save." "Where am I going to get that type of money?" Hoggie asked. Canvy answered, "From sponsors, investors, and loans. Canvy then explained...

1. Sponsors are people who give you money that you don't have to pay back.

2. Investors give you money so they can own a piece of your business.

3. A loan is money that you borrow. When a bank gives you a loan, you must pay them back...

...The funny thing about it is, that you have to pay them back more than they gave you." Hoggie smiled as he took notes.

Finally, Hoggie and Canvy decided to ask Hoggie's parents to be sponsors. Hoggie was excited to show his parents his business plan. He told his parents that he had completed his goal. "Hoggie," his Mom said, "What do you know about a business?" Hoggie explained what he learned while working on his plan and told them all about it. Hoggie's parents were amazed at all Hoggie had done. His Mom asked, "Hoggie, how did you learn all this?" "From the canvas you got me," said Hoggie. "His name is Canvy. He's my mentor." Hoggie's parents were so excited they didn't even realize that Hoggie was talking to a canvas. "We are so proud of you. You worked very hard, so we would like to support you by giving you a $2500 sponsorship." Hoggie was excited. "Thank you, now I just need $3000 more!" he said.

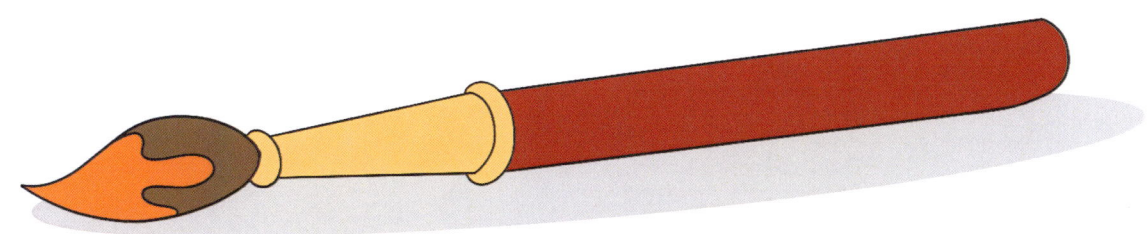

"Now, let's think about marketing moves," Canvy said. "Who are we selling to, and where will we sell the products at." "My customers will be kids, adults, and anyone looking for art and clothes," said Hoggie. "I can put the art in other businesses like storefronts, my websites, art galleries, and office spaces." "Great!" said Canvy. "Write that down." When Hoggie finished writing, Canvy said, "Now we have to get the word out about your business. Let's do some networking all over!"

"Wait... What's networking?" Hoggie asked. Canvy answered. "It's when you go out and meet people who can help you grow your art. Come on, Hoggie. Put on your best outfit, and let's go network!"

So, in a blink of an eye, Canvy and Hoggie were off to a networking event for entrepreneurs. Hoggie met an art gallery owner at the event, and the owner invited him to come down to see his gallery! Hoggie and Canvy were so excited they couldn't wait to visit his gallery! Then, they remembered that they still needed to raise the money to pay for the supplies.

Later that week, Hoggie decided to sell some ice cream to raise more money. He asked his brother, Gordo, to help him with a stand. Hoggie, Gordo, and Canvy made signs and flyers to set up the ice cream stand. After selling a lot of ice cream, they went home to count their money. They made $1200 in one day. Canvy told the boys that they had to split the money they made since they were business partners. So that meant they each got $600 a piece.

Hoggie went back to his parents with his head held down. "What's wrong, champion?" said Hoggie's dad. Hoggie said, "I still don't have enough money!!" Hoggie lifted his head and said, "I can ask my family and friends to help. I know they will!"

Hoggie and his Mom started calling family and friends. Everyone was excited to help Hoggie. After adding up all his money from family and friends, Hoggie was still $50 short, so he decided to take out a small business loan. He got the $50 and reached his goal.

When Hoggie and Canvy got to the art store, there were hundreds of supplies for his project. Now that Hoggie had all the money he needed, it was time to pick out his supplies! Hoggie picked out an iPad, an apple pencil, paint, canvases, and a case that he liked.

The gallery owner asked Hoggie for the business' name. Hoggie thought about it, then told Canvy his idea for the name of the business. "Let's call it 'Hoggie's World.' Canvy thought about it and said, "Hoggie's World. Yeah, I like the sound of that." "Hoggie's World it is!" the gallery owner said as he wrote the business name on the order form. And boom, Hoggie's first art piece was in an art gallery.

Canvy was a great mentor to Hoggie, and Hoggie put in a lot of hard work. Because of this, Hoggie's World became a huge success! Every week, Hoggie would collect money from his sales of artwork. He just kept getting more and more money! He used his money to buy clothes, video games, and other things! Hoggie's World was so successful that other kids wanted to learn from him. Soon, Hoggie began teaching other kids how to become successful artists too! Everyone was impressed and proud of Hoggie for what he had done. Hoggie proved to everyone that kids can become anything they want with hard work and good mentorship.

Just a kid, a canvas, and a dream!

Jordan Arnell Evans also known as "Hoggie" (Born April 28, 1990, in Sandusky, Ohio) is an American artist, illustrator, graphic designer, painter, videographer, and creator of the "Art Jordan" brand. Jordan is best known for his artwork for the start of the 2016 NBA season (the Cleveland Cavaliers NBA Championship year), which featured an art illustration that included Lebron James, Kyrie Irving, Tristan Thompson, and Iman Shumpert. In 2022, He created work for ESPN College Gameday Morning show set. Jordan has designed and exhibited his creations nationally at various venues, including art for celebrities and professional athletes. Jordan's services include album art, company logos, concert posters, and event flyers.

BUSINESS PLAN

Name of your business?

_____

1. What will you be selling?

_____

2. How much will you sell it for?

_____

3. How much money do you need to start this business?

_____

4. Who are you selling this too? (Kids, Adults, Friends, ect.)

_____

5. What are your goals for this business?

_____

Best Design and Business Plan Hoggie will design the logo for you.
So send to artjordanceo@gmail.com

It's your turn to design. Be creative and think big!

Draw your Logo Design
(Include Business Name, and Tagline)

HOGGIE'S World

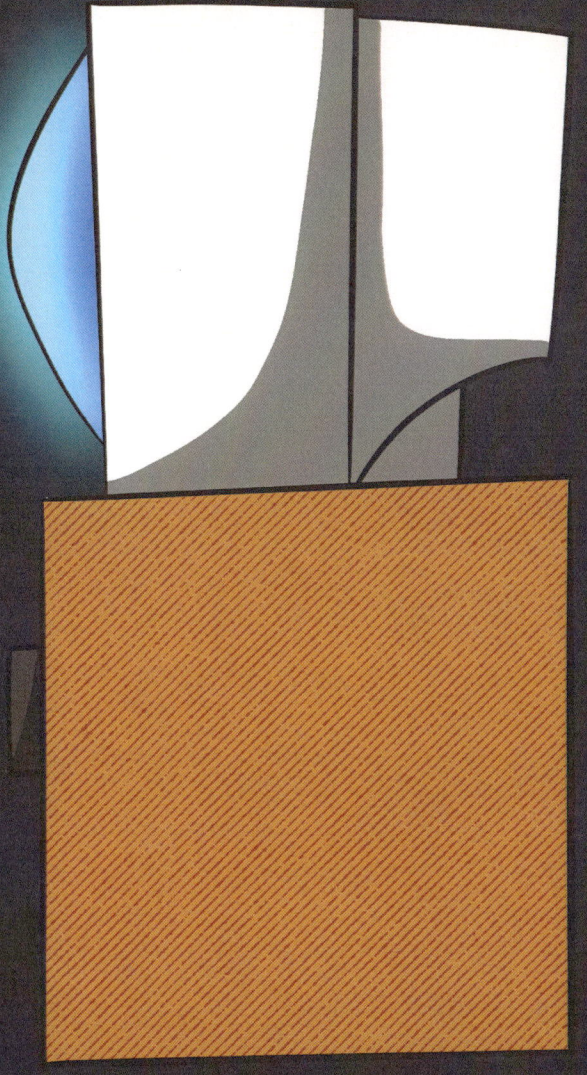

Printed in the USA
CPSIA information can be obtained
at www.ICGtesting.com
LVRC090815190424
777824LV00015B/45